CW01096123

THE WORLD'S TOP C

Feeling fit and healthy combined with epicurean enjoyment perfectly harmonize with tasty organic wines.

JACQUES TREMBLAY
MARIE-ANGE GAGNON
FRÉDÉRIC TREMBLAY

GSP
GLOWING SHADOW PRODUCTIONS INC.

Other Glowing Shadow Productions – *glowingshadow.com*:

The Sexteens – Teen novels – *sexteen4u.com*
Benjamin and Rosie – Children's books – *benrosie.glowingshadow.com*
Tremblay du Saguenay – *tremblay.glowingshadow.com*

First Edition

Published by Glowing Shadow Productions Inc., RR4, Gananoque, Ontario, K7G 2V6
glowingshadow.com
wine.glowingshadow.com

The World's Top Organic Wines
ISBN : 978-0-9810322-2-1

Printed in the United States of America for American distribution
Printed in the United Kingdom for European distribution

CONTENTS

Preface

It is a great pleasure to release this first edition of The World's Top Organic Wines. This book is geared for all wine lovers who want to discover and appreciate the world of organic wines.

This publication comments on fifty-one organic wines chosen from twelve different countries, fifteen unique varietals and twenty-three different blends including Chianti.

My wife and I discovered organic wines about ten years ago. We gradually moved in that direction. The transition was facilitated by the exceptional quality that we discovered bottle after bottle: vivid color, distinctive aroma, exquisite taste and munificent finale. In addition, organic wine is definitely a plus for our health and well-being thanks to grapes produced in sustainable agriculture free of all chemical influence, and in the winery, a better selection of yeast and no synthetic chemical fining agents.

Our passion for organic and macrobiotic wine is led by the taste first, and we gain, as a bonus, a better health.

Enjoy reading, and savor these outstanding wines!

How to use this book?

The top dark green header

The top green header shows the name of the wine followed by the country and the region where the wine was produced according to organic standards. It also indicates the varietal or blended varieties; the categories as well as red, rosé or white; the best time to enjoy it and the vintage.

The light green side

Tasting features:

The tasting features reflect our team's observations. We tried all wines presented in this guide during the last year. Evaluating the color, nose, taste and much more is a process that appeals to senses, judgement and feelings, which is obviously a very personal interpretation. To avoid any kind of bias or subjectivity, our team appraises wines using some guidelines such as serving them at the recommended temperature, always using the same kind of glass and keeping all samples in a good cellar before consumption. We've had a great pleasure tasting those fine gifts from nature. It is your turn now!

Serve with:

These are some suggestions based on reading and experiencing. According to your favorite dishes, you will certainly select the best organic wine to fire up a feast. Be audacious in matching wine and food, you will impress yourself as well as your friends.

Particularities:

This piece specifies the certification and any relevant technical information such as varietals, winery's history, serving temperature and aging or cellaring process.

Availability:

Some wines are very easy to find year round such as, Bonterra, Frey, Full Circle, Nature Perrin and Sonop. Depending on the country and region where you live, they may be available just once a year. You can usually buy organic wines from you local store. Otherwise, some wineries sell their products online. Our philosophy is when we find a wine that we really like, we quickly buy a few more bottles just to make sure we will have enough to wait for the next release. In fact, some organic wines are often offered in specific limited edition and it greatly influences availability.

Sugar content and Sulphur level:

The sugar content and sulphur level reflect the information supplied by the producer in accordance with the certified organization.

It is important for some people to know the sugar content. We've used this scale that ranges from Extra Dry to Sweet: XD, D, MD, M, MS, S.

Sulphur is an essential concept of organic winemaking. It is important to note that high levels of sulphites may significantly contribute to headaches or hangovers. The certified organizations regulate and enforce rigorous standards that include the use of sulphur. Red wines naturally contain antioxidants and generally present a lower amount of SO_2 than rosé and white ones. As a guideline, an organic wine with more than 10mg/l must be labeled as "containing sulphites". Under 60mg/l, it is considered low; under 10mg/l, it is only a trace. In preparation for this book, we select wines presenting 50mg/l or less. In comparison, a conventional non-organic wine often displays a level above 400mg/l.

Alcohol:
This note refers to the alcohol percentage indicated on the bottle.

Prices:
This section indicates a low and a high price. Prices may vary according to the region were you live, taxes and transportation. We bought a bottle of Frey at $9.50 in the US and the same product cost us $17.00 in Canada.

Conclusion:
It is certainly our favorite section to write as we emphasize on what impressed us the most. We took this opportunity to express our passion for these lovely wines, trying to briefly target what is remarkable and distinctive about each one.

Our Rating / Your Rating:
We rate from 1 to 5, five being the best quote. No mention under 2.75 was given in this book merely because all the wines we evaluated were at least over average. Producing an organic wine implies high expectations, from the vineyard to the winery. Therefore, it sparkles in an astonishingly winey experience. It would have been unfair to any producer mentioned in this book to receive a rating under 2 considering the quality of the product offered.

To conclude, we've tried to indicate a fair appreciation considering flavor, taste, general feeling and price. Your appraisal is also very valuable. So, we invite you to make your own, and mark it in the book. You can also share your rating at <u>wine.glowingshadow.com</u>, which will be reflected in the next publication.

What are organic wines?

The organic wine process starts first in organic vineyards where the ecosystem and biodiversity are entirely respected. This noble art continues in the winery where the approach follows rigorous ethical standards in techniques and cellaring.

Producing an organic wine begins in the vineyard
The vines grow in a healthy soil well-enriched with compost such as organic manure, bone meal, fish meal and humus. These natural fertilizers make the soil a mineral-rich medium. It consequently brings to the fruits a better resistance to diseases. Therefore, the organic grapes used for making organic wines are free from synthetic chemical fertilizers, pesticides, herbicides and fungicides. Most organic certifications require that the vineyard be free of all chemicals for a period of at least three years.

Biodiversity and soil maintenance are essential to succeed in organic farming. The producers protect the vines by planting local grasses between the rows, which is a great option to fight weeds, provide nutrients to the soil and restrain erosion. The geese are welcomed guests as they are beneficial to the vineyard, eating unwanted weeds.

Companion plants are more than an eye-catching outlook; they help in the growth of vines, attracting beneficial insects to repel harmful pests. For example, in California, prune trees and blackberry bushes are introduced in the grape fields to attract the tiny wasp Anagrus as a biological control of the very destructive grape leafhoppers. Sometimes, ladybirds are released to naturally control aphids.

Producing an organic wine also takes place in the winery
The organic winemakers take specific care and follow special techniques to transform grapes into a great wine.

In certified organic wine productions, the winemakers clean the equipment with ozone or another natural product. They use wild or ambient yeast for the fermentation process. One of the major points is that no synthetic chemical fining agents are permitted such as Bentonine, PVPP, Silicon dioxide (Kiesselsol). In non-organic productions, these chemicals are unfortunately used to artificially remedy to some lacks: tannin reduction, color adjustment, clarity and stability, quality impairment and volume of lees. The organic process implies that the filtration is kept to a minimum, retaining precious beneficial elements such as tannins, resveratrol and antioxidants.

Biodynamics
The vignerons follow the moon cycle. Some producers adopt a biodynamic practice, which is a method that ensures a healthy balance between the soil, vine plants and environment. Wine growers believe that there is an improvement in the color, aroma and concentration of the grapes in a biodynamic vineyard.

Carbon-neutral

The carbon-neutral practice moves forward slowly. Businesses that are certified manage their CO_2 emissions to protect the habitat. Grove Mill, a producer from New Zealand, is a leader in this technique.

Fair Trade and Sustainable agriculture

According to Wikipedia, *Fair trade is an organized social movement and market-based approach to empowering developing country producers and promoting sustainability. Fair trade's strategic intent is to deliberately work with marginalized producers and workers in order to help them move from a position of vulnerability to security and economic self-sufficiency.* Some farms and vineries are proud to be certified Fair Trade such as Las Lomas and Sonop.

Why choose an organic wine?

According to Richard Béliveau, Ph. D., the resveratrol contained in red wine helps in the prevention of cancer. According to Ultimate Foods for Ultimate Health, the flavonoids found in red wine, which act as antioxidants, may help to prevent damage to the cardiovascular system. Alcohol is good if taken in small quantity. These authors suggest 5 oz (145 mL) to 10 oz (290 mL) a day depending on your weight.

Taking into consideration the benefits for our health and the necessity to avoid trace of chemical pollutants, it is certainly a very wise choice to drink organic wines. There is no doubt for us, we deserve the best. And you?

Our eleven favorites

We were impressed by many wines that we appraised, but we would like to mention some that we unanimously evaluate as exceptional.

We tried Sonop wines from South Africa: a red, a rosé and a white (pages 51-52-54). Those three are absolutely delectable, and the "Rosé de Pinotage" is the apotheosis. You can definitely trust Sonop's products.

From Italy, we need to mention Barbera del Monferrato (page 44) and San Michele a Torri (page 47). The latter, a Chianti, with Sangiovese as the dominant variety in the blend, is very well balanced and rich in flavor. This wine always makes our party successful. The first Italian mentioned reveals all the aromas and the fantastic taste present in this amazing varietal, Barbera. This red is a match to its great renown.

Greece surprised us with Filiria (page 41), a blend of two rare varieties, Xinomavro and Negoska. Already delicious now, but suitable for aging. We also need to bring up a superb rosé produced by Spiropoulos (page 42) called Meliasto that is mouthwatering in spite of its unusual color. We often savor a Spiropoulos the first day of holiday to set a laid-back ambiance.

We were impressed by Frey's wines from the US. Their Syrah (page 61), low in acidity, was so appreciated that we snatched a few bottles to enrich our cellar. Frey demonstrates, beyond any doubt, that California produces great organic wines.

From France, we discovered a rare organic sparking wine, the Delmas (page 31). We made that one our celebration companion. Still from France, Domaine Saint-Rémy (page 35), a Gewurztraminer, is more that an interesting wine. This phenomenal white wine bursts with flavor and nose. It tastes much sweeter than the level of sugar indicated. To conclude, Perrin often offers the "Nature Perrin" (page 38) organic wine. It is a fantastic red, resulting from a blend of Grenache and Syrah, that is always seductive year after year. Don't hesitate, you will be charmed!

BUDINI
ARGENTINA- MENDOZA

MALBEC
RED   DRINK NOW 1 -2 YEARS   **2005**

TASTING FEATURES:
A dark purple color with aromas and flavors of red currants. Medium finish.

SERVE WITH:
Barbecued beef, steak and tomato-based dishes. Also a good companion for a cheese sandwich.

PARTICULARITIES:
Although not certified organic yet, the grapes are produced according to the code of sustainable agriculture, protecting the environment.

AVAILABILITY: Once a year.

SUGAR CONTENT: XD

FREE SULPHUR / ALCOHOL
Not specified   13.5%

PRICES:
$9.00 to $13.00   750 ml

CONCLUSION:
Terrific value. Easy to enjoy. An excellent opportunity to try the Malbec varietal. We savored one and we bought a six-pack the day after.

OUR RATING: * * * * ¼
YOUR RATING: ___/5

13

DEMETER

AUSTRALIA- ROBINVALE

CHARDONNAY / CHENIN BLANC / SAUVIGNON BLANC
WHITE　　　DRINK NOW OR HOLD 5 -7 YEARS　　　**2005**

TASTING FEATURES:
This distinctive blend shows a light golden color. The nose is rich in fruity aromas, keeping a crisp finish in the mouth.

SERVE WITH:
Great with vegan/vegetarian dishes or white fish. Appreciated with unripened cheeses. Also fantastic with goat cheese and spinach frittata.

PARTICULARITIES:
Certified biodynamic, following enhanced organic methods, according to the standards of the Research Institute. A screw-cap wine. Contains a preservative.

AVAILABILITY: Once a year.

SUGAR CONTENT: D

FREE SULPHUR / ALCOHOL
Not specified　　　　　　　13%

PRICES:
$15.00 to $21.00　　　　　750 ml

CONCLUSION:
This wine's finish exults zingy fruitiness. It is an experience to appreciate this dry white wine with relatives or friends.

OUR RATING:　　* * ¾
YOUR RATING:　　___/5

14

SALENA

AUSTRALIA- RIVERLAND

GRENACHE / SYRAH / MOURVÈDRE
ROSÉ   DRINK NOW 1 -2 YEARS   2007

TASTING FEATURES:
Strong raspberry aromas. This soft and fruity rosé has a very appealing structure, full-bodied and mouth-filling, finishing with a gentle cleansing dryness.

SERVE WITH:
A tasty match for stir-fry vegetables, grilled prawns or steamed mussels. The right personality to create a harmonious ambiance with traditional Bouillabaisse.

PARTICULARITIES:
Certified by Australian Organic. Ready to enjoy while fresh and young.

AVAILABILITY: Once a year.

SUGAR CONTENT: D

FREE SULPHUR / ALCOHOL
Very low, 15 mg/l   13.5%

PRICES:
$16.00 to $22.00   750 ml

CONCLUSION:
Its bright fruity color will please as much the aficionado as the novice. Spoil yourself with this gift from Australia.

OUR RATING: * * * * ¼
YOUR RATING: ___/5

EMILIANA COYAM
CHILE - COLCHAGUA VALLEY
SYRAH / CARMENERE / CABERNET SAUVIGNON / MERLOT / PETIT VERDO

RED　　　DRINK NOW OR HOLD 5 -7 YEARS　　　**2005**

TASTING FEATURES:
Unique wine with a lush fruity color and subtle oak flavors. Long finish with low acidity.

SERVE WITH:
Organic meat, spelt pastas, cheese and seafood dishes.

PARTICULARITIES:
Coyam is a blended wine made through sustainable agriculture that lets reach the maximum expression of the terroir's conditions. Biodynamically and organically certified by IMO. You can enjoy now, but suitable to mature further by cellaring.

AVAILABILITY: Once a year.

SUGAR CONTENT: XD

FREE SULPHUR / ALCOHOL
Very low, 17 mg/l　　　14.5%

PRICES:
$18.00 to $25.00　　　750 ml

CONCLUSION:
Vibrant and delicious. Well-priced considering the level of quality. A must!

OUR RATING:　　* * * *
YOUR RATING:　　___/5

LAS LOMAS
CHILE - D.O. MAULE VALLEY

CHARDONNAY
WHITE   DRINK NOW 1 -2 YEARS   **2007**

TASTING FEATURES:
Balanced fruit-forward wine with a soft finish. Delicate aromas.

SERVE WITH:
Steamed mussels, grilled chicken, wild fish topped with a mango salsa or crab in a cream sauce.

PARTICULARITIES:
Vina Lomas de Cauqenes was the first organic winery in Chile. A Fair Trade product and organically certified by IMO.

AVAILABILITY: Once a year.

SUGAR CONTENT: D

FREE SULPHUR / ALCOHOL
Trace, 9 mg/l   13.9%

PRICES:
$12.00 to $17.00   750 ml

CONCLUSION:
Terrific as much for an aperitif as for a main plate.

OUR RATING: * * * * ¼
YOUR RATING: ___/5

NATURA
CHILE - CENTRAL VALLEY

CABERNET SAUVIGNON
RED   **DRINK NOW OR HOLD 5 -7 YEARS**   **2006**

TASTING FEATURES:
This full-flavored wine, rich in beneficial tannins, reveals aromas of wild flowers. Well-balanced.

SERVE WITH:
Organic lamb, red meat, pastas with red sauces and strong cheeses.

PARTICULARITIES:
Certified by IMO Switzerland. Emiliana is one of the largest organic growers with more than 1700 acres of biodynamic vineyard land. The producer uses alpacas and goats to weed the vineyard. Suitable to mature further by cellaring.

AVAILABILITY: Few times a year.

SUGAR CONTENT: XD

FREE SULPHUR / ALCOHOL
Very low, 25 mg/l   14%

PRICES:
$12.00 to $17.00   750 ml

CONCLUSION:
Great choice for meat lovers. Delicious!

OUR RATING: * * * *
YOUR RATING: ___/5

NATURA CARMENERE
CHILE - COLCHAGUA VALLEY

CARMENERE
RED   DRINK NOW 1 -2 YEARS   **2005**

TASTING FEATURES:
This world-class Carmenere has notes of ripe cherries and plums as well as a medium-long finish.

SERVE WITH:
Pastas, pizza, cheeses, sardines and meat.

PARTICULARITIES:
Originally planted in the Médoc, region of Bordeaux, Carmenere is now very rare in France. The world's largest area planted with this variety is in Chile. Certified by IMO Switzerland. This organic viticulture leans toward the true expression of the Chilean terroir.

AVAILABILITY: Once a year.

SUGAR CONTENT: XD

FREE SULPHUR / ALCOHOL
Very low, 21 mg/l   14%

PRICES:
$12.00 to $17.00   750 ml

CONCLUSION:
Distinctive flavors that will flabbergast your guests. Carmenere tastes so delicious. Quite rare but amazing!

OUR RATING: * * * * ¼
YOUR RATING: ___/5

NOVAS EMILIANA
CHILE - COLCHAGUA VALLEY
CARMENERE / CABERNET SAUVIGNON
RED
DRINK NOW 1 -2 YEARS
2005

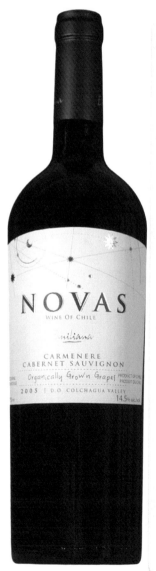

TASTING FEATURES:
A crimson robe with aromas of spices, dark prune and strawberry lead to complex flavors and an oaky finish, stabilizing the ripe tannin and acidity.

SERVE WITH:
It makes a fine partner for barbecued burgers, gourmet pizza, vegetarian sausages and grilled salmon.

PARTICULARITIES:
Organic and biodynamic by IMO. Viñedos Emiliana was the first Chilean vineyard that voluntarily adopted the international standards for the care and protection of the environment. This wine aged for 12 months in American oak casks.

AVAILABILITY: Few times a year.

SUGAR CONTENT: XD

FREE SULPHUR / ALCOHOL
Trace, 7 mg/l   14.5%

PRICES:
$12.00 to $17.00   750 ml

CONCLUSION:
Terrific value and very attractive.

OUR RATING: * * * * ¼
YOUR RATING: ___/5

NOVAS EMILIANA
WINEMAKER'S SELECTION
CHILE - CASABLANCA VALLEY
CHARDONNAY / MARSANNE / VIOGNIER

WHITE   DRINK NOW OR HOLD 3 -5 YEARS   **2006**

TASTING FEATURES:
This wine has an interesting yellow color presenting intense aromas of citric fruit, apricot and jasmine complemented by mineral notes, all intermingled with elegant touches of mocha and toffee. Juicy on the palate, it is pleasantly balanced between acidity and alcohol, has a good volume and a finish that lingers enjoyably.

SERVE WITH:
Delicious with grilled chicken, barbecued shrimp, whitefish, sole in a chives cream sauce and artichoke salad. Also perfect with rice pudding.

PARTICULARITIES:
Certified organic by IMO. Enjoy now. It will also improve with 3-5 years in a cellar.

AVAILABILITY: Few times a year.

SUGAR CONTENT: XD

FREE SULPHUR / ALCOHOL
Trace, 7 mg/l   14,5%

PRICES:
$16.00 to $22.00   750 ml

CONCLUSION:
One of the most famous white organic wines!

OUR RATING: * * * ¾
YOUR RATING: ___/5

CHÂTEAU CHAVRIGNAC
FRANCE - BORDEAUX
MERLOT / CABERNET FRANC / CABERNET SAUVIGNON / MALBEC
RED DRINK NOW 1 -2 YEARS **2005**

TASTING FEATURES:
Aromas and flavors of cherry, plum, cassis and earth tone. Palatable, appetizing and a long finish.

SERVE WITH:
Grilled portobello mushrooms, fish, seafood or cheese.

PARTICULARITIES:
Silver Medal Paris 2006. Serve at a temperature of-12-14°C / 53-57°F. Certified organic by Ecocert.

AVAILABILITY: Once a year.

SUGAR CONTENT: XD

FREE SULPHUR / ALCOHOL
Very low, 12 mg/l   13%

PRICES:
$11.00 to $16.00   750 ml

CONCLUSION:
Low price for an excellent Bordeaux. An exceptional blend to add to your cellar. We enjoyed Château Chavrignac for the last few years and we noticed consistent quality.

OUR RATING: * * * * ½
YOUR RATING: ___/5

CHÂTEAU LAUBARIT
FRANCE - BORDEAUX

MERLOT / CABERNET SAUVIGNON

RED　　　**DRINK NOW 1 -2 YEARS**　　　**2002**

TASTING FEATURES:
A delightful bouquet of red berry fruit and plum, and a soft, racy flavor. The immediate impression on the nose is sweet fruit and spicy oak.

SERVE WITH:
Excellent match with salads, foie gras, raclette, meat dishes and cheese.

PARTICULARITIES:
This land is built on a porous limestone base topped with iron-rich loess. Controlled by the French Certification Authority Ecocert. One of the rare biodynamic vineyards in Bordeaux certified by Demeter.

AVAILABILITY: Once a year.

SUGAR CONTENT: XD

FREE SULPHUR / ALCOHOL
Low　　　　　　　　12%

PRICES:
$13.00 to $18.00　　　　750 ml

CONCLUSION:
Excellent price for a great Bordeaux. A full-flavored blend to enrich your cellar.

OUR RATING: ＊＊＊＊
YOUR RATING: ___/5

CHÂTEAU PUY D'AMOUR
FRANCE - BORDEAUX

MERLOT - DOMINATED 80%
RED   **DRINK NOW** 1 -2 YEARS   **2005**

TASTING FEATURES:
The 80% dominating merlot brings roundness and fruit to this wine. Aromas and flavors of wild berries. Palatable long finish.

SERVE WITH:
The best food matches are toasted meats, game birds and soft cheeses. Great with grilled Halloumi cheese.

PARTICULARITIES:
Produced through a biological wine-making process. Decant the wine two hours before tasting and serve at a temperature of 16-18°C / 61-64°F.

AVAILABILITY: Once a year.

SUGAR CONTENT: XD

FREE SULPHUR / ALCOHOL
Very low, 27 mg/l   13.5%

PRICES:
$16.00 to $22.00   750 ml

CONCLUSION:
Enjoy this sensational wine. You will feel like you are sitting at a terrace in France on a sunny day.

OUR RATING: * * * *
YOUR RATING: ___/5

CHÂTEAU VIEUX-GEORGET

FRANCE - BORDEAUX

CABERNET SAUVIGNON 50% / MERLOT 25%
CABERNET FRANC 25%

RED **DRINK NOW** OR **HOLD 5 -7 YEARS** **1998**

TASTING FEATURES:
A rich, full bodied red wine, deliciously smooth and generously fruity. The nose reveals strong hints of Merlot. On the palate, good structure and well-balanced supple tannins.

SERVE WITH:
A recommended partner to mature cheeses, all vegetarian dishes, lamb and red meats.

PARTICULARITIES:
This fine claret is produced entirely organically, stipulated by the UNIA (Union Nationale Interprofessionnelle de l'Agrobiologie). Serve at a temperature of 16°C / 61°F. Can be drunk during the year or also age for 5 to 7 years.

AVAILABILITY: Once a year.

SUGAR CONTENT: XD

FREE SULPHUR / ALCOHOL
Very low, 12 mg/l   12.5%

PRICES:
$15.00 to $21.00   750 ml

CONCLUSION:
It's always inspiring and delectable, year after year. An epicurean Bordeaux!

OUR RATING: * * * * ½
YOUR RATING: ___/5

ROUGE NATURE
FRANCE - BORDEAUX / GIRONDE

CABERBET SAUVIGNON / MERLOT
RED   DRINK NOW 1 -2 YEARS   2002

TASTING FEATURES:
Classic round and fruity with low acidity. This Bordeaux features aromas of cherry and red currant with a long finish.

SERVE WITH:
Organic beef or lamb, ratatouille, cheddar cheese.

PARTICULARITIES:
Organically certified by Ecocert. Benoit Valérie Calvet blended organic Cabernet Sauvignon from one of his parcels with organic Merlot from another vigneron. Ready to drink now or within 24 months.

AVAILABILITY: Once a year.

SUGAR CONTENT: XD

FREE SULPHUR / ALCOHOL
Trace, 9 mg/l   12.1%

PRICES:
$11.00 to $16.00   750 ml

CONCLUSION:
Excellent value for a good Bordeaux. Easy to drink on any occasion. A wine offering something simple, but perfectly balanced.

OUR RATING: * * * ¾
YOUR RATING: ___/5

CHÂTEAU LE MONASTÈRE
FRANCE - CÔTE DE BOURG

MERLOT / CABERNET SAUVIGNON
RED   DRINK NOW 1 -2 YEARS   **2002**

TASTING FEATURES:
A deliciously smooth full-bodied red wine. It has intense, vibrant red and black fruit characters and a rich opulent taste with a full mouthfeel.

SERVE WITH:
Excellent with a wide variety of spicy or peppery dishes such as casseroles, lamb and piquant steak.

PARTICULARITIES:
Organic wine certified by Ecocert. Serve at room temperature.

AVAILABILITY: Once a year.

SUGAR CONTENT: XD

FREE SULPHUR / ALCOHOL
Low   12%

PRICES:
$12.00 to $17.00   750 ml

CONCLUSION:
A fantastic French wine. Aphrodisiac and romantic. Perfect for lovers.

OUR RATING: * * * * ¼
YOUR RATING: ___/5

CHÂTEAU PECH-LATT

FRANCE - MIDI, CORBIERES

CARIGNAN
RED   DRINK NOW 1 -2 YEARS   **2006**

TASTING FEATURES:
This crispy and fruity Carignan has a juicy tang on the finish.

SERVE WITH:
Organic sirloin steaks. Indian cuisine, especially with paneer.

PARTICULARITIES:
Organic wine certified by Ecocert. The monks from Pech-Latt planted the first vineyard of the chateau in the year 784. Today's owners of Chateau Pech-Latt are proud of the exceptional quality of their wines.

AVAILABILITY: Once a year.

SUGAR CONTENT: XD

FREE SULPHUR / ALCOHOL
Very low, 26 mg/l   14%

PRICES:
$14.00 to $19.00   750 ml

CONCLUSION:
A very good French wine. Lovely Carignan-based beauty.

OUR RATING: * * * * ¼
YOUR RATING: ___/5

CHÂTEAU ROUBIA
FRANCE - MINERVOIS

CARIGNAN / GRENACHE / MOURVÈDRE / SYRAH

RED   DRINK NOW 1 -2 YEARS   **2005**

TASTING FEATURES:
Château Roubia is enticing with its aromas of blackberry and wild flowers. Soft and ample tannins with medium acidity.

SERVE WITH:
Grilled steak, gourmet vegetarian spicy sausages and pizzas.

PARTICULARITIES:
One of the oldest wineries of Languedoc. Now owned by Grotti-Mestre family who continues the traditional culture. Certified by Ecocert.

AVAILABILITY: Once a year.

SUGAR CONTENT: XD

FREE SULPHUR / ALCOHOL
Very low, 12 mg/l   13%

PRICES:
$9.00 to $13.00   750 ml

CONCLUSION:
Very good value in taste and price. Don't hesitate for a daily choice.

OUR RATING: * * * ¾
YOUR RATING: ___/5

CHÂTEAU SAINT GERMAIN
FRANCE - COTEAUX DU LANGUEDOC

SYRAH 75% / **GRENACHE** 20% / **MOURVÈDRE** 5%

RED   **DRINK NOW** or **HOLD 3 -5 YEARS**   **2004**

TASTING FEATURES:
This deep, ruby-purple wine displays thoroughly unique, exotic, liqueur-like aromas of ripe blackberries and orange peel. On the palate, its velvety texture and abundant fruit are buttressed by soft but ample tannins.

SERVE WITH:
This great wine accompanies well carrots, rutabagas and beets, strong cheeses, red meats and gourmet sausages.

PARTICULARITIES:
Organically and biodynamically certified by Ecocert. Vines were first planted by the Romans over 2000 years ago. Enjoy now or it will also improve with 3-5 years in a cellar.

AVAILABILITY: Once a year.

SUGAR CONTENT: XD

FREE SULPHUR / ALCOHOL
Trace, 6 mg/l   14%

PRICES:
$14.00 to $19.00   750 ml

CONCLUSION:
This lovely wine brings you a sea breeze from the Mediterranean. Amazing color and tannins. Voluptuous perfume!

OUR RATING: * * * * ½
YOUR RATING: ___/5

DELMAS

FRANCE - BLANQUETTE DE LIMOUX

MAUZAC 80% / **CHARDONNAY** 20%
WHITE SPARKLING **DRINK NOW** 1 -2 YEARS   **2002**

TASTING FEATURES:
A dry, rich and golden-colored wine. Seductive aromas of nutmeg and fragrant jasmine flowers. This mellow sparkling wine features citrusy and Golden Russet apple flavors. Interesting long finish of agave nectar.

SERVE WITH:
Hors-d'oeuvres, Brie, hard cheeses, creamy pasta, calamari, oysters, shellfish and sushi.

PARTICULARITIES:
In 1531, the monks who were cultivating the golden grapes Mauzac, called Blanquette, discovered by accident natural sparking wine: the first brut in the world. Organically certified by Ecocert.

AVAILABILITY: Once a year.

SUGAR CONTENT: D

FREE SULPHUR / ALCOHOL
Low   12%

PRICES:
$19.00 to $26.00   750 ml

CONCLUSION:
Either for a romance dinner, leisure or celebration. A naturally fizzy white to leave your guests speechless.

OUR RATING: * * * * *
YOUR RATING: ___/5

31

DOMAINE CAZES - EGO
FRANCE - CÔTES DU ROUSSILLON

SYRAH 40% / **GRENACHE** 40% / **MOURVÈDRE** 20%

RED   **DRINK NOW** 1 -2 YEARS   **2006**

TASTING FEATURES:
The nose and taste are dominated by wild red fruits with black licorice and sour cherry on a long finish.

SERVE WITH:
Young rabbit with tomatoes and basil, foie gras, chicken curry, cake with almonds.

PARTICULARITIES:
Organically certified by Ecocert. Biodynamically certified by Concert. For the last ten years, Domaine Cazes has been using biodynamic viticulture methods. Made completely in stainless steel.

AVAILABILITY: Once a year

SUGAR CONTENT: XD

FREE SULPHUR / ALCOHOL
Trace, 9 mg/l   13.5%

PRICES:
$18.00 to $25.00   750 ml

CONCLUSION:
A breathtaking blend that will make you feel good. A glass of this great wine before sleep will spoil you.

OUR RATING: * * * *
YOUR RATING: ___/5

DOMAINE DE LA SAUVEUSE
FRANCE - CÔTES DE PROVENCE

CABERNET / SYRAH / GRENACHE / MOURVÈDRE
RED   DRINK NOW 1 -2 YEARS   **2005**

TASTING FEATURES:
The palate is full-bodied, tannic, well balanced with a nose of black fruits. This flavorful Provençal wine exhibits a ruby color with a succulent tightly woven mouthfeel.

SERVE WITH:
A perfect choice for all dishes prepared with olive oil. Grilled lamb skewers, salad and nuts, pastas and pizza.

PARTICULARITIES:
Certified organic by Ecocert. Winner of Prix des Vinalies Nationales 2007. Aged in French oak barrels for 12 months. Malolactic fermentation process. Serve at a temperature of 16/18°C / 61/64°F.

AVAILABILITY: Once a year

SUGAR CONTENT: XD

FREE SULPHUR / ALCOHOL
Very low, 13 mg/l   13%

PRICES:
$17.00 to $23.00   750 ml

CONCLUSION:
It is a distinctive wine for festive occasions. Amazing with pesto dishes.

OUR RATING: * * * *
YOUR RATING: ___/5

33

DOMAINE DES COCCINELLES
FRANCE - CÔTES DU RHÔNE

GRENACHE / SYRAH / MOURVÈDRE / CINSAULT
RED
DRINK NOW 1 -2 YEARS
2005

TASTING FEATURES:
An intense purplish-red color with a delicacy of spices, cassis and blueberries. Rich in mouth, this wine develops a powerful scent of fruits. A medium-bodied with soft tannins and moderate acidity.

SERVE WITH:
Casseroles, stews, vegetable pies, cabbage dishes, lamb, cream cheese and grilled fish.

PARTICULARITIES:
Certified organic by Qualité France.

AVAILABILITY: Once a year

SUGAR CONTENT: D

FREE SULPHUR / ALCOHOL
Very low, 12 mg/l   14%

PRICES:
$10.00 to $15.00   750 ml

CONCLUSION:
This traditional wine is a real drinking pleasure. We've tried many vintages, and Domaine des Coccinelles is always excellent year after year.

OUR RATING: * * * *
YOUR RATING: ___/5

DOMAINE SAINT-RÉMY
FRANCE - ALSACE

GEWURZTRAMINER
WHITE   DRINK NOW 1 -2 YEARS   **2006**

TASTING FEATURES:
Strong and powerful aromas of rose, lychee, meadow flowers and a variety of spices. Pleasant and tasty in mouth with a particularly long finish. Sweet feeling for a dry wine.

SERVE WITH:
Great match for any spicy cuisine. Suitable with raw oysters. Terrific as a dessert wine with Canadian maple taffy on snow.

PARTICULARITIES:
Certified by Ecocert.

AVAILABILITY: Once a year

SUGAR CONTENT: D

FREE SULPHUR / ALCOHOL
Very low, 27 mg/l   13.5%

PRICES:
$15.00 to $21.00   750 ml

CONCLUSION:
Excellent value for money. You will enjoy sipping this seductive and aphrodisiac white in the afternoon or at dinner. Gewurztraminer's fans will be flabbergasted.

OUR RATING: * * * * *
YOUR RATING: ___/5

35

DOMAINE TERRES BLANCHES
FRANCE - PROVENCE

CARIGNAN / MOURVÈDRE / SYRAH
RED   DRINK NOW or HOLD 5 -7 YEARS   **2001**

TASTING FEATURES:
Crimson ruby color, red fruit jam nose, licorice and wooded touch with blackberry and raspberry aromas, well balanced wine. Ample mouthfeel with long finish.

SERVE WITH:
Braised chicken, goose, vegetarian stew, garlicky pasta and ratatouille.

PARTICULARITIES:
Controlled by Quality France. Organic and biodynamic creed. Matured for 18 months in oak casks. Enjoy now or up to 7 years of cellaring.

AVAILABILITY: Once a year.

SUGAR CONTENT: XD

FREE SULPHUR / ALCOHOL
Trace   13.5%

PRICES:
$20.00 to $28.00   750 ml

CONCLUSION:
This hearty wine from Provence brings the sun to your glass. Don't worry about the harvest year; we taste it every year and we are always amazed.

OUR RATING: * * * *
YOUR RATING: ___/5

DOMAINE TERRES BLANCHES
FRANCE - PROVENCE

COUNOISE / MOURVÈDRE / GRENACHE NOIR / SYRAH
ROSÉ   DRINK NOW 1 -2 YEARS   **2002**

TASTING FEATURES:
This excellent blend slightly varies each year to give a well-balanced wine with floral aromas, good acidity and medium-full body. Lovely fruit sweetness on the nose, enriched by crisp strawberry, herbs and also a hint of melon. The palate is very juicy.

SERVE WITH:
Perfect choice for appetizers or happy hour. Suitable with seafood or all cheeses.

PARTICULARITIES:
Controlled by Quality France. Organic and biodynamic creed. Domaine Terres Blanches has been organic since 1970.

AVAILABILITY: Once a year

SUGAR CONTENT: D

FREE SULPHUR / ALCOHOL
Low   14%

PRICES:
$11.00 to $16.00   750 ml

CONCLUSION:
This versatile rosé is an excellent companion for any cuisine you will serve at a garden party.

OUR RATING: * * * * ¼
YOUR RATING: ___/5

NATURE PERRIN
FRANCE - CÔTES DU RHÔNE

GRENACHE / SYRAH
RED   DRINK NOW 1 -2 YEARS   **2005**

TASTING FEATURES:
Lively, with aromas of ripe red berries, tasty licorice, a hint of pepper, complex spicy fruit in the mouth and a deliciously long finish.

SERVE WITH:
Meat, brown rice, pasta, all types of cheese and spicy dishes - especially those with a Mediterranean flavor.

PARTICULARITIES:
It is so called because it comes from organically grown grapes, without any chemical treatment in the vineyard. Ecocert. Not to be confused with "Réserve Perrin", which is not organic.

AVAILABILITY: Once a year.

SUGAR CONTENT: XD

FREE SULPHUR / ALCOHOL
Trace, 9 mg/l   13%

PRICES:
$12.00 to $17.00   750 ml
$7.00 to $11.00   375 ml

CONCLUSION:
Excellent value for money. Also available in half bottles. This organic wine reflects the Perrin et Fils' high standards. Our guests always appreciate it. Widely available.

OUR RATING: * * * * ¾
YOUR RATING: ___/5

PUJOL
FRANCE - CÔTES DU ROUSSILLON
SYRAH 40% /MOURVÈDRE 20% /CARIGNAN30% / GRENACHE 10%

RED   DRINK NOW 1 -2 YEARS   2001

TASTING FEATURES:
A purple color with a nose of scarlet berries. Smooth in tannins and very spicy with a zesty finish.

SERVE WITH:
Grilled red meats, tuna steaks and aged cheeses.

PARTICULARITIES:
This 2001 edition won a Gold Medal in Paris in 2003. The Pujol family grows Syrah, Mouvedre, Carignan and Grenache. Jose Pujol aims at producing the perfect wine each year.

AVAILABILITY: Rare.

SUGAR CONTENT: XD

FREE SULPHUR / ALCOHOL
Trace   13%

PRICES:
$12.00 to $17.00   750 ml

CONCLUSION:
Tasting a Pujol is a unique experience. If you find one, buy it!

OUR RATING: * * * * ¼
YOUR RATING: ___/5

XAVIER
FRANCE - CÔTES DU RHÔNE

BLEND OF MORE THAN 10 DIFFERENT VARIETIES

RED DRINK NOW 1 -2 YEARS **2003**

TASTING FEATURES:
An outstanding cuvée with an impressive red color that exhales a palette of intense aromas. As soon as it touches the palate, it reveals spices, rounded with chocolate and a long finish.

SERVE WITH:
This complex wine may enrich a wide variety of food.

PARTICULARITIES:
This wine, a Vacqueyras appellation, is certified by Ecocert. Xavier Vignon has the reputation of being the "master of blends".

AVAILABILITY: Few times a year.
SUGAR CONTENT: XD
FREE SULPHUR / ALCOHOL
Low   13.5%

PRICES:
$13.00 to $18.00   750 ml

CONCLUSION:
The fact that this wine bears my grandfather's name aroused my curiosity. We were so impressed by Xavier's blends that we've tried many different editions. These wines are an astonishingly good value for money. Add to your cellar.

OUR RATING: * * * * ¼
YOUR RATING: ___/5

FILIRIA
GREECE

XINOMAVRO 50% / **NEGOSKA** 50%

RED   **DRINK NOW OR HOLD 5 -7 YEARS**   **2003**

TASTING FEATURES:
Xinomavro assures smooth aging, while Negoska increases the alcohol level, softens the characteristics of Xinomavro and offers to the wine its rich, red color. Negoska also brings intensity for a long final.

SERVE WITH:
Pesto pizza, octopus and Halloumi cheese.

PARTICULARITIES:
This wine is aged in French oak barrels for at least one year. Certified by the Certification and Inspection Organisation of Organic Products DIO.

AVAILABILITY: Once a year.

SUGAR CONTENT: XD

FREE SULPHUR / ALCOHOL
Low   13%

PRICES:
$17.00 to $23.00   750 ml

CONCLUSION:
Remarkable wine from very rare varieties. The taste can only improve further with aging. Definitely an upscale wine!

OUR RATING: * * * * ¾
YOUR RATING: ___/5

MELIASTO SPIROPOULOS
GREECE - PELOPONNESE

MOSCHOFILERO

ROSÉ **DRINK NOW 1 -2 YEARS** **2005**

TASTING FEATURES:
The lovely salmon color combined with full aromas of rose attar are very seductive. Well-balanced with low acidity; the flavors of true rose and strawberry caramel are a delight for the palate.

SERVE WITH:
It matches a huge variety of food and particularly international dishes.

PARTICULARITIES:
This rosé is organically produced from a noble unique varietal "Moschofilero". These grapes grow at an altitude of 650 m. Serve at a temperature of 10/12°C / 50/54°F, offering a harmonious complement to a plethora of gastronomic cuisines.

AVAILABILITY: Once a year.

SUGAR CONTENT: D

FREE SULPHUR / ALCOHOL
Trace, 9 mg/l 11.5%

PRICES:
$12.00 to $17.00 750 ml

CONCLUSION:
You may certainly enjoy by itself or as a top leader for your next degustation.

OUR RATING: * * * * *
YOUR RATING: ___/5

TSANTALI
GREECE - HALKIDIKI

CABERNET SAUVIGNON

RED   **DRINK NOW** 1 -2 YEARS   **2003**

TASTING FEATURES:
The nose of this fine offering is redolent of mint with a powerful palate of cassis, blueberry and herbaceous cherry.

SERVE WITH:
Calamari, paella, red meat, fettuccine Alfredo, vegetarian chick peas lasagna, navy beans and feta cheese.

PARTICULARITIES:
Gold Medal at the 2007 Concours Mondial de Bruxelles. Organically Certified by DIO.

AVAILABILITY: Once a year.

SUGAR CONTENT: XD

FREE SULPHUR / ALCOHOL
Low   14.5%

PRICES:
$15.00 to $21.00   750 ml

CONCLUSION:
A reasonable acidity level makes this robust wine a drinking pleasure. This inky wine with a high level of resveratrol will fulfill your expectations in taste and health.

OUR RATING: * * * *
YOUR RATING: ___/5

BARBERA DEL MONFERRATO NUOVA CAPPELLETTA MINOLA

ITALY - PIEDMONT

BARBERA

RED   **DRINK NOW 1 -2 YEARS**   **2004**

TASTING FEATURES:

This wine offers a distinctive fragrance of fresh dark berries. Deep color with low tannins, full-bodied and a high level of acidity with notes of cherries.

SERVE WITH:

Artisanal Italian cheeses, risotto, grilled Bocconcini and Pesto sandwich, and all spicy dishes. Fantastic with bagna cauda, a famous warm dip typical of Piedmont usually prepared with anchovies, crushed garlic and olive oil.

PARTICULARITIES:

Organic and biodynamic certified by Demeter since 1984. Barbera is one of the most planted varietals in Italy.

AVAILABILITY: Once a year

SUGAR CONTENT: XD

FREE SULPHUR / ALCOHOL

Low, 30 mg/l   13%

PRICES:

$20.00 to $28.00   750 ml

CONCLUSION:

Incontestably fancy, absolutely posh. One of our favorites when we feel for a flavorful wine.

OUR RATING: * * * * *
YOUR RATING: ___/5

CASTELLO DI RAPALE
ITALY - TUSCANY

CHIANTI (SANGIOVESE 90% AND CANAIOLO 10%)

RED   **DRINK NOW 1 -2 YEARS**   **2001**

TASTING FEATURES:
This vermillion wine with aromas of wild flowers is fruity, full-bodied and unveils hints of spices.

SERVE WITH:
Great match with pizzas, pastas, mushrooms, turkey and organic red meat. Amazing with aged cheeses.

PARTICULARITIES:
Organically grown grapes certified by Associazione Suolo e Salute.

AVAILABILITY: Once a year.

SUGAR CONTENT: XD

FREE SULPHUR / ALCOHOL
Very low, 17 mg/l   13.5%

PRICES:
$15.00 to $21.00   750 ml

CONCLUSION:
Lively and vibrant, keeping its innate character. Enjoy it on a cold winter evening while watching a hockey game. It is one of my daughter's favorites. A mellow Chianti.

OUR RATING: * * * *
YOUR RATING: ___/5

PRATELLO CATULLIANO LUGANA
ITALY - LOMBARDY

TREBBIANO DI LUGANA
WHITE   DRINK NOW 1 -2 YEARS   **2006**

TASTING FEATURES:
The glacial plain and the moderating cool breezes of Lake Garda create wines that are pleasingly aromatic. Fruity and floral olfactory sensations are perfectly balanced with aromas of peaches, apples, pears and white rose petals. In the mouth, it is soft and well rounded.

SERVE WITH:
Excellent accompaniment to a wide assortment of culinary dishes. In particular, it matches well with seafood, pasta, risotto, grilled fish or herbed mushroom-based dishes. Better served at 12-14°C / 53-57°F.

PARTICULARITIES:
Organically grown grapes certified by Istituto Mediterraneo Certificazione.

AVAILABILITY: Once a year

SUGAR CONTENT: XD

FREE SULPHUR / ALCOHOL
Low, 33 mg/l   12.5%

PRICES:
$12.00 to $17.00   750 ml

CONCLUSION:
This extra dry white wine will seduce you, and all your guests.

OUR RATING: * * * *
YOUR RATING: ___/5

SAN MICHELE A TORRI
ITALY - TUSCANY, FLORENCE

CHIANTI
RED   DRINK NOW 1 -2 YEARS   **2005**

TASTING FEATURES:
A well-balanced organic fancy Chianti with juicy red fruit and aromatic crushed strawberry flavors. An exclusive cherry color and a very nutty aroma. Good tannins and medium finish.

SERVE WITH:
Pastas with tomato sauce, roast meats and cheeses. Awesome with fusion cuisine.

PARTICULARITIES:
The production of this Chianti follows the local agricultural traditions where respect for the environment and quality of the wines are a priority. Serve at room temperature.

AVAILABILITY: Once a year

SUGAR CONTENT: XD

FREE SULPHUR / ALCOHOL
Trace, 9 mg/l   12.5%

PRICES:
$13.00 to $18.00   750 ml

CONCLUSION:
This wine pops Sangiovese's cherry flavors. It is a love potion for the ones who believe in seduction.

OUR RATING: ✱ ✱ ✱ ✱ ✱
YOUR RATING: ___/5

SANTA VENERE
ITALY - CALABRIA, CIRO

GAGLIOPPO
RED   DRINK NOW OR HOLD 5 -7 YEARS   **2006**

TASTING FEATURES:
Gaglioppo produces a light red wine that is full-bodied and high in tannins. A tantalizing aroma of fresh cranberries. The ending is very light on the palate.

SERVE WITH:
It pairs well with hamburgers, cold cuts and Italian dishes.

PARTICULARITIES:
This wine was fermented in stainless steel with a few months of bottle aging. It sees no oak. Certified organic.

AVAILABILITY: Once a year.

SUGAR CONTENT: XD

FREE SULPHUR / ALCOHOL
Trace, 9 mg/l   13.5%

PRICES:
$13.00 to $18.00   750 ml

CONCLUSION:
It is a great value, especially if you are seeking something a bit different.

OUR RATING: * * * *
YOUR RATING: ___/5

TERRA VERDE
MOLDOVA - CAHUL

CABERNET SAUVIGNON

RED   **DRINK NOW 1 -2 YEARS**   **2004**

TASTING FEATURES:
This is a solid Cab with an aftertaste of pure black currants with notes of vanilla and sweet herbs. Astonishing nose of unsweetened chocolate and black currant. Medium finish.

SERVE WITH:
Pasta or legumes with tomato dishes, grilled rib-eye steak topped with mushrooms. Also good with grilled salmon.

PARTICULARITIES:
Certified organic by SGS. Moldova, a land of green hills and no pollution, has the largest expanse of organic vineyards in the world. Long tradition for over 2000 years. Long ago, their wines have most notably graced the table of the Russian Tsars.

AVAILABILITY: Once a year

SUGAR CONTENT: XD

FREE SULPHUR / ALCOHOL
Not specified   13.5%

PRICES:
$9.00 to $13.00   750 ml

CONCLUSION:
This is a seductive Cabernet at an equally attractive price.

OUR RATING: * * * ¾
YOUR RATING: ___/5

GROVE MILL
NEW ZEALAND - MARLBOROUGH

PINOT GRIS

WHITE DRINK NOW, NOT SUITABLE FOR CELLARING　　**2007**

TASTING FEATURES:
This Pinot Gris has a straw yellow color; it has a ripe scent with slightly sweet nectarine and lychee flavors.

SERVE WITH:
Antipasti, Caesar salad, fish, paella, seafood quiche, fruit pie and soft cheeses.

PARTICULARITIES:
This winery is a leader in sustainable agriculture. In 2006, Grove Mill was proud to be the first carbon-neutral winery in the world. A screw-cap wine.

AVAILABILITY: Once a year.

SUGAR CONTENT: D

FREE SULPHUR / ALCOHOL
Low　　　　　　　　　　13.5%

PRICES:
$15.00 to $21.00　　　　750 ml

CONCLUSION:
It is always a noble pride to drink a silky delicate wine produced in harmony with the environment.

OUR RATING:　　* * * *
YOUR RATING:　　___/5

SONOP
SOUTH AFRICA- WESTERN CAPE

CABERNET SAUVIGNON

RED   **DRINK NOW** 1 -2 YEARS   **2006**

TASTING FEATURES:
Intense green pepper and black currant aromas. Soft tannins on the palate are followed by a fruity and long finish.

SERVE WITH:
Pair with whole grain pasta in a meat or tofu sauce.

PARTICULARITIES:
Certified organic by the USDA. Also certified Fair Trade.

AVAILABILITY: Once a year.

SUGAR CONTENT: XD

FREE SULPHUR / ALCOHOL
Trace, 9 mg/l   15.5%

PRICES:
$10.00 to $15.00   750 ml

CONCLUSION:
Very good value in taste and price. A palatable and melt-in-your-mouth Cab. A great gift from Nature. It is, beyond any doubt, a wonderful combination of taste and health.

OUR RATING: * * * * ¾
YOUR RATING: ___/5

51

SONOP
SOUTH AFRICA- WESTERN CAPE

PINOTAGE
ROSÉ OF PINOTAGE　　**DRINK NOW 1-2 YEARS**　　**2006**

TASTING FEATURES:
Dark pinkish color. Fruity cherry aromas. Intense strawberry flavors. Dry and extremely refreshing.

SERVE WITH:
Excellent choice to relax with cheeses, tortillas, bruschetta and braised fillet of sole with almonds.

PARTICULARITIES:
A true reflection of the South African Western Cape's organic terroir. Certified organic by the USDA. Fair Trade.

AVAILABILITY: Once a year.

SUGAR CONTENT: D

FREE SULPHUR / ALCOHOL
Low　　　　　　　　　　12.5%

PRICES:
$10.00 to $15.00　　　　　750 ml

CONCLUSION:
We enjoy sipping in warm summer afternoons. So fruity and mouthwatering! Sonop, either Red or Rosé, is always my son's first choice.

OUR RATING:　　＊ ＊ ＊ ＊ ＊
YOUR RATING:　　___/5

52

UPLAND
SOUTH AFRICA- WELLINGTON

CABERNET SAUVIGNON
RED   DRINK NOW 1 -2 YEARS   **2003**

TASTING FEATURES:
Flavors of black fruits, spice and vanilla.
Silky tannins and a long finish.

SERVE WITH:
A perfect choice for barbecued ribs or any
burgers. Awesome with dark chocolate.
Great to accompany Quebec's cuisine such
as poutine, tourtière and oreilles de crisse.

PARTICULARITIES:
Silver Medal by Michelangelo International
Wine Awards. This organic farm is a
haven for a rich variety of bird life and is
a shining example of biodiversity, which
ensures that this wine didn't "Cost the
Earth." Certified organically grown
grapes SGS.

AVAILABILITY: Once a year.

SUGAR CONTENT: D

FREE SULPHUR / ALCOHOL
Trace, 6 mg/l   13%

PRICES:
$13.00 to $18.00   750 ml

CONCLUSION:
Like many South African wines, it's a very
good value in taste and price.

OUR RATING: * * * * ¼
YOUR RATING: ___/5

53

WINDS OF CHANGE
SOUTH AFRICA- WESTERN CAPE

CHARDONNAY
WHITE   DRINK NOW 1-2 YEARS   **2007**

TASTING FEATURES:
This Chardonnay with a dazzling vivid color has juicy pineapple and kiwi fruit flavors. The nose shows a clean fruity and floral bouquet.

SERVE WITH:
It pairs well with oysters, salmon, lemon sole, trout, veal and chicken. This wine will enrich sheep and goat cheeses.

PARTICULARITIES:
Inspired by history, Winds of Change exemplifies the vibrancy, spirit, courage and hope of South Africa. Certified organic by the CU; also a Fair Trade product.

AVAILABILITY: Few times a year.

SUGAR CONTENT: D

FREE SULPHUR / ALCOHOL
Very low, 11 mg/l   13%

PRICES:
$10.00 to $15.00   750 ml

CONCLUSION:
Another top-notch wine from Sonop Village. This chardonnay is intense and radiant. Unbelievable price!

OUR RATING: * * * * *
YOUR RATING: ___/5

ALBET I NOYA LIGNUM

SPAIN- PENEDÈS, CATALONIA

CABERNET SAUVIGNON 22% / **CARINYENA** 39% /
GARNATXA (ALSO KNOWN AS **GRENACHE**) 39%

RED   **DRINK NOW** I -2 YEARS   **2003**

TASTING FEATURES:
Its deep red color makes it rich in
resveratrol. Fruit flavors with vanilla
tones from the wooden casks offering a
full-body and a long finish. Old vines
Garnatxa and Carinyena form around
80% of this blend, giving a good vibrant
fruit quality backed up by spicy tannins.

SERVE WITH:
Quiche, shrimp salad, pastas, fish soup,
beef, cheeses and chocolate cake.

PARTICULARITIES:
Certified organic by CCPAE. This wine
is aged in Tennessee oak barrels. Better
served at 17°C / 63°F.

AVAILABILITY: Once a year.

SUGAR CONTENT: XD

FREE SULPHUR / ALCOHOL
Low   13.5%

PRICES:
$13.00 to $18.00   750 ml

CONCLUSION:
Mouthwatering. A luscious and fragrant
wine at a low price.

OUR RATING: * * * *
YOUR RATING: ___/5

ALBET I NOYA

SPAIN- PENEDÈS, CATALONIA

MERLOT 75% / **PINOT NOIR** 25%

ROSÉ   **DRINK NOW** 1 -2 YEARS   **2004**

TASTING FEATURES:
Bright strawberry red color with nose of exploding wild fruits.
Balanced acidity.

SERVE WITH:
Refreshing with aperitif, Antipasti, cucumber sandwiches, chicken,
cheeses. It matches well Catalan cuisine. Amazing with vanilla ice
cream.

PARTICULARITIES:
Certified organic by CCPAE. No picture available at the time of
the publication. According to Richard Béliveau, Ph. D., Pinot Noir is
one of the best anticancer varietals.

AVAILABILITY: Once a year.

SUGAR CONTENT: XD

FREE SULPHUR / ALCOHOL
Low   12.5%

PRICES:
$13.00 to $18.00   750 ml

CONCLUSION:
You can always trust Albet i Noya's wines. A terrific rosé that
will complement your cellar. A very lively and engaging one. It
is my daughter's favorite for a romantic dinner with her husband.

OUR RATING: * * * * ½
YOUR RATING: ___/5

DOMINIO BASCONCILLOS
SPAIN- BURGOS - RIBERA DEL DUERO

TINTA DEL PAÍS (TEMPRANILLO)
RED   DRINK NOW OR HOLD 4 - 6 YEARS   **2004**

TASTING FEATURES:
This varietal is ruby red with aromas and flavors of wild berries, plum and vanilla. It surrounds the palate in an intensely fruity perfume. Full-bodied and persistent.

SERVE WITH:
Vegetarian or meat stew, beef bourguignon, paella and duck. Also excellent with Spanish style dishes such as tapas, a plate of olives, marinated mushrooms, Chorizo sausage, prawns and mixed seafood.

PARTICULARITIES:
Aged 12 months in 60% French oak barrels and 40% American. Certified organic by DUERO.

AVAILABILITY: Once a year.

SUGAR CONTENT: XD

FREE SULPHUR / ALCOHOL
Trace, 6 mg/l   14.5%

PRICES:
$19.00 to $26.00   750 ml

CONCLUSION:
Indisputably a high-class wine. Suitable for cellaring.

OUR RATING: * * * * ¼
YOUR RATING: ___/5

BONTERRA

U.S.A. CALIFORNIA- MENDOCINO COUNTY

CABERNET SAUVIGNON

RED   DRINK NOW I -2 YEARS   **2005**

TASTING FEATURES:
A full mouthfeel with a generous lingering finish. Juicy red cranberry flavors with spicy tones and slight vanilla notes.

SERVE WITH:
Lamb, beef stew, veal, vegetarian lasagna, quiche, lima beans or lentils.

PARTICULARITIES:
California Certified Organic Farmers CCOF. Available year round.

AVAILABILITY: Easy to find.

SUGAR CONTENT: D

FREE SULPHUR / ALCOHOL
Very low, 18 mg/l   12.09 %

PRICES:
$18.00 to $25.00   750 ml

CONCLUSION:
For someone who appreciates a lively acidity. An interesting wine to discover.

OUR RATING: * * *
YOUR RATING: ___/5

BONTERRA

U.S.A. CALIFORNIA- MENDOCINO COUNTY

CHARDONNAY

WHITE   DRINK NOW I -2 YEARS   **2006**

TASTING FEATURES:
The exciting impression of crème brûlée twists into dreamy aromas of juicy and lemony fruits. The raciness of the acids provides a refreshing and appealing finish.

SERVE WITH:
Antipasti, avocado with shrimps, seafoods, oysters, crab and lobster.

PARTICULARITIES:
California Certified Organic Farmers CCOF. This Chardonnay contains light touches of Viognier, Roussane and Muscat. Available year round.

AVAILABILITY: Easy to find.

SUGAR CONTENT: D

FREE SULPHUR / ALCOHOL
Very low, 24 mg/l   13.6%

PRICES:
$14.00 to $19.00   750 ml

CONCLUSION:
It is a great one especially if you enjoy a sharp-tasting wine.

OUR RATING: * * * ¾
YOUR RATING: ___/5

BONTERRA
U.S.A. CALIFORNIA- MENDOCINO COUNTY

SYRAH
RED   DRINK NOW 1-2 YEARS   **2005**

TASTING FEATURES:
The inviting burgundy color combined with aromas of glamorous tangerine blossoms are irresistible. Silky medium tannins. The layers of taste are highlighted by flavors of blue and black fruits.

SERVE WITH:
Thai dishes, Indian cuisine, smoked salmon, peppery steak and aged cheeses.

PARTICULARITIES:
California Certified Organic Farmers CCOF. Malolactic fermentation. Available year round.

AVAILABILITY: Easy to find.

SUGAR CONTENT: D

FREE SULPHUR / ALCOHOL
Very low, 10 mg/l   14%

PRICES:
$18.00 to $25.00   750 ml

CONCLUSION:
It will please all robust wine lovers. Very tasty with a long finish.

OUR RATING: * * * * ¼
YOUR RATING: ___/5

FREY

U.S.A. CALIFORNIA- REDWOOD VALLEY

SYRAH
RED   DRINK NOW 1 -2 YEARS   **2006**

TASTING FEATURES:
A full-bodied, opulent wine with a deep ruby color and flavors of plum, cocoa, blackberry, cedar notes and a long crisp finish.

SERVE WITH:
Roasted lamb, Kamut organic pasta and seafoods.

PARTICULARITIES:
Biodynamic. GMO-free. Stellar Certification Services. It is widely known that Frey Vineyards is the oldest and largest exclusively organic winery in the USA.

AVAILABILITY: In USA, available year round. May vary in other countries.

SUGAR CONTENT: XD

FREE SULPHUR / ALCOHOL
Trace, 6 mg/l   13.7%

PRICES:
$9.00 to $16.00   750 ml

CONCLUSION:
One of the best for its high quality. Fragrant, luxurious and elegant. A must!

OUR RATING: * * * * ¾
YOUR RATING: ___/5

FULL CIRCLE
U.S.A. CALIFORNIA- HOPLAND

CABERNET SAUVIGNON
RED   DRINK NOW I -2 YEARS   **2005**

TASTING FEATURES:
A complex and flavorful Cab. Ripe fruit aromas with a hint of spice leading to pleasing flavors of berry preserves with a touch of oak.

SERVE WITH:
Spelt pastas, lamb, aged cheeses and pure chocolate.

PARTICULARITIES:
Certified organic by CCOF. It is a screw-cap bottle.

AVAILABILITY: In USA, available year round. May vary in other countries.

SUGAR CONTENT: XD

FREE SULPHUR / ALCOHOL
Low   13.5%

PRICES:
$8.00 to $14.00   750 ml

CONCLUSION:
Good wine at a very low price. Don't hesitate to enjoy often. A Full Circle of delectation!

OUR RATING: * * *
YOUR RATING: ___/5

TRUE EARTH
U.S.A. CALIFORNIA- ST.HELENA, NAPA
CABERNET SAUVIGNON / MERLOT / SYRAH
RED   **DRINK NOW 1-2 YEARS**   **2007**

TASTING FEATURES:
Brilliant carmine color with a softly earthy aroma. The taste is sharp on palate, well-balanced and exceptionally singular.

SERVE WITH:
Red meat, wild rice, strong-flavored cheeses and spicy dishes such as the ones from the Caribbean. Ideal for haute cuisine.

PARTICULARITIES:
Certified by California Organic Farmers.

AVAILABILITY: Once a year.

SUGAR CONTENT: D

FREE SULPHUR / ALCOHOL
Very low, 17 mg/l   13.5%

PRICES:
$14.00 to $19.00   750 ml

CONCLUSION:
We recommend it if you like dry European-style reds. "Taste first" is the philosophy of this organic winery.

OUR RATING: * * * *
YOUR RATING: ___/5

FONSECA PORTO TERRA PRIMA
PORTUGAL - DOURO VALLEY, PORT

ORGANIC GRAPES FROM DOURO VALLEY
PORT WINE   **Released in 2007**

TASTING FEATURES:
Rich, unctuous and fruity port. It is robust and characterful in a classy ruby style with flavors of blueberry, cherry and plum. Treacly notes.

SERVE WITH:
Enjoy with aged hard cheeses; Stilton, Cheddar, Gouda, Brie, Camembert de Portneuf and Gruyere cheeses. Serve also as a dessert wine.

PARTICULARITIES:
Certified organic by Ecocert. The Douro region has a microclimate that is perfect for the growth of special grapes to make the famous Port wine. Better served at 18-20°C / 64-68°F.

AVAILABILITY: Once a year.

SUGAR CONTENT: S (10)

FREE SULPHUR / ALCOHOL
Trace 6 mg/l   20%

PRICES:
$22.00 to $29.00   750 ml

CONCLUSION:
If you feel for a sturdy port, just agreeably sweet, it's an irresistible outstanding wine from Oporto.

OUR RATING: * * * * ¾
YOUR RATING: ___/5

JUNIPER GREEN ORGANIC LONDON DRY GIN
ENGLAND, UK
2007

CHARACTERISTICS:
It is the world's first organic London Dry Gin. It is made from organic grain, juniper, coriander, angelica and savory. 100% gluten free. It is a great choice for the traditional martini.

PARTICULARITIES:
Certified Organic by USDA, Soil Association Organic Standards, Certified CCOF Farmers. You will find more info on the Web link   http://www.maisonjomere.com/aboutjuniper.htm

ALCOHOL   43 %

PRICES: $24.00 TO $38.00   750 ML

Picture from the website.

Index by Categories

Index by Countries

Index by Names

Index by Varietals

Specific Varietals:

Index by Blends

Blends:

Bibliography

http://en.wikipedia.org/wiki/Barbera   44

http://en.wikipedia.org/wiki/Fair_trade   10

http://www.african-terroir.co.za/fairtrade.html   51, 52, 54

http://www.african-terroir.co.za/sonop_cellar.html   51, 52

http://www.barberadelmonferrato.it/new/   44

http://www.bonterra.com/   58, 59, 60

http://www.cadre.qc.ca/arrep/Dossier%20Colloque%202006/
la_lutte_au_cancer_par_l.htm   10, 56

http://www.ecocert.com/

http://www.freywine.com/freywine/   61

http://www.lcbo.ca/main/en.shtml

http://www.maisonjomere.com/aboutjuniper.htm   65

http://www.perrin-et-fils.com/beaucastel/2007/05/perrin_et_fils__l.html   38

http://www.scribd.com/doc/2187990/The-Story-Behind-Winemaking-
Fining-And-Fining-Agents   9

http://www.uark.edu/depts/ifse/grapeprog/articles/nmc14wg.pdf   9

Pearson, Liz, and Mairlyn Smith. "Ultimate Foods for Ultimate Health."
Whitecap (2007): 98-99.   10

Printed in the United States
1291LVUK00001B